WHAT DO YOU KNOW?
Gyles Brandreth

Illustrated by Terry Burton

CAROUSEL BOOKS
A DIVISION OF TRANSWORLD PUBLISHERS LTD.

This personal log book belongs to:

Full name:

Address:

Telephone number:

Age:

Signature:

Date:

BEFORE YOU
RACE AWAY...

Most of us really know far more about a lot of things than we give ourselves credit for. The trouble is that we tend to forget how much we know and often, when we're asked to prove how brainy we are, we get flustered and give the idea that we don't know anything. And that's why this book is so important.

Here, in your hands, is a record (or it will be a record once you've been through it) of everything you know about hundreds of different things. It's a record of what you know about the world you live in and the world that people lived in in the past. It's a record of your knowledge of important subjects like science, the natural world and space travel, and it's an even more important record of what you know about the things you enjoy at the moment. Why more important? Because they're the ones that are most likely to change as you change. And in this case the most important subject is **you** — that's why we've left you to finish the book.

Inside you'll find lots and lots of questions. Most of them you'll be able to answer straightaway, so just fill in the blanks provided. If you're really brainy you'll be able to answer them all with no difficulty. But there are a few which will make you think a bit (we've given you clues to help you along, so you ought to be able to answer these after you've scratched you head for a while).

If you get really stuck and you can't possibly answer a question there's no need to give up. There's no need to get someone else to answer it for you. All you'll have to do is to go to a reference book and look the answer up for yourself — there's a list at the back. That way you'll have the satisfaction of finding the answer, and you'll learn something new at the same time. (If you want to be really honest and see how much you did know, when you look at this book in the future, you ought to fill in the answers in two different colours — one colour for the ones you answered without looking anything up, the other for the ones you had to look up).

The important thing is to end up with all the answers completed. This will then be a record of just some of thousands of things that you know at the moment. Of course you'll learn lots more later on. But later on too, you'll be able to get out this book to check on how much you knew when you were younger. You never know, it might even cheer you up if life's being a bit awkward!

So, to start with there are two sections devoted entirely to **you**, but as you'll see at the end, the final section deals with you too. But before you start getting to grips with your future, see how you get on with the present. . .

YOU AND YOUR WORLD

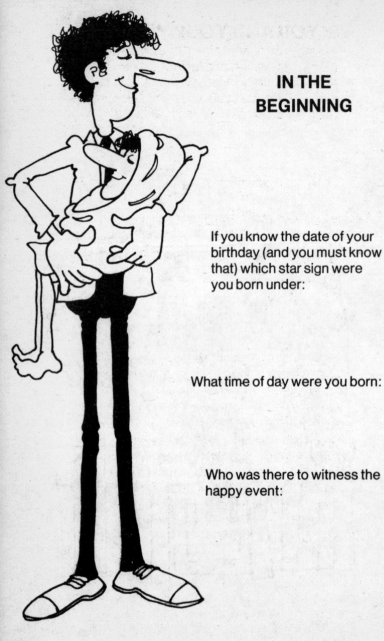

IN THE
BEGINNING

If you know the date of your birthday (and you must know that) which star sign were you born under:

What time of day were you born:

Who was there to witness the happy event:

10

Why did your parents choose your first name — were you named after a relation, a close friend, the doctor, or a famous person? One father got carried away and named his baby after all eleven players in a winning football team — so why did you get your name:

What about your other forenames (the other names before your surname) why were you given those, if any:

Everyone has a surname and you probably share yours with thousands, if not millions of other people. But why have you got that name? What does it mean? It may tell you something about your ancestors. People who used to grind corn used to be called Miller. People with names which begin with Mac- or Mc- often came from Scotland or Ireland. Where do you think your ancestors might have come from and what might they have done? (You might find a clue in a *Dictionary of Surnames* in a library).

YOUR MUM AND DAD

Where did your Mum and Dad get married
(girls usually get married near their own
homes):

What time of year did they get married (are
there photographs of their wedding which give
you a clue about the season, or do you know
when they celebrate their wedding
anniversary?):

Some women still keep their original name after they get married. But most wives take their husband's surname. A girl's name before she is married is called her maiden name. What was your mum's:

Where did they live when they were your age:

MUM   **DAD**

Where did your parents go to school:

MUM   **DAD**

What exams did they take at school:

MUM   **DAD**

Did they have any education or training after school:

MUM   **DAD**

What qualifications did they get from this (qualifications are sometimes given as initial letters like B.Sc. which means Bachelor of Science, or H.N.C. which means Higher National Certificate):

MUM   **DAD**

If you've got brothers and sisters you'll know when they were born, but do you know where (start with the eldest and list them by age):

How many nieces and nephews do your parents have between them:

YOUR GRANDPARENTS

Lots of people have started taking a great interest in their family histories, so to start you off on your investigations, do you know where your grandparents were living when your Mum and Dad were born:

MUM'S PARENTS   **DAD'S PARENTS**

What jobs did your grandfathers do when they were your Dad's age:

MUM'S DAD   **DAD'S DAD**

Did either of your grandmothers go out to work:

MUM'S MUM　　　　**DAD'S MUM**

Your grandparents were most likely alive during the Second World War. Do you know what they were doing in it? Were your grandfathers soldiers, sailors, or airmen, or were they busy working on the home-front:

MUM'S DAD　　　　**DAD'S DAD**

And what about your grandmothers, were they serving in the armed forces, or were they working at home:

MUM'S MUM　　　　**DAD'S MUM**

You have two sets of grandparents. How many sets of great-grandparents did you have:

Your mother's parents are sometimes called your *maternal* grandparents. Do you know what your father's parents are called (you have to change one letter in *maternal* to get the right word):

YOUR HOME

If you live in a street, or a road with a name, do
you know why it's called that? Some streets
and roads are named after famous people,
some are named after towns and cities, some
are named after rivers and others are named
after nearby places. What's the name of your
road and street, and why is it called that:

You're bound to know your address, but what's your postcode (postcodes are very helpful because they help the Post Office pin-point your home. If you don't know your postcode your nearest post office will tell you what it is):

Now let's put you on the map.
Which of these cities is the nearest to your home (if you can, try and list them in order starting with the nearest and ending with the one furthest away):

CITIES	NEAREST TO YOUR HOME
London	1.
Glasgow	2.
Bristol	3.
Manchester	4.
Southampton	5.
Birmingham	6.

Now let's look at your home itself. How would you describe it? Is it a bungalow, a flat or a house:

Which way does the front of your home face? Does it face south, west, east, or north? How can you tell? Which side catches the sun's beams when the sun rises? The sun rises in the east, so that side of your home must face east:

What is your home built out of. Is it built out of bricks, out of stone, out of wood, or out of concrete:

What is the roof made from. Is it made from tiles or from slates, or does it have a flat roof with some other material to keep out the rain and the wind:

What are the windows like in your home. Do you have double-glazing? Do you have sash windows, which slide up and down, or do you have casement windows, which open on hinges (try and answer without having a look):

You know that hot water comes out of the hot taps. How is it heated (the answer may be connected with the sort of cooker your Mum uses. If she cooks on gas, your hot water is probably heated by gas too. On the other hand if you have a large tank outside your house, this means that your hot water is heated by burning oil):

YOUR GARDEN OR YOUR NEAREST PARK

On which side of your home is the garden or the park? Is it to the north, the south, to the east, or to the west? (remember the side on which the sun rises, that will give you your clue):

Are there any trees growing in your garden, or in the nearest park? If there are, do they keep their leaves all the year round, or do they lose them in the autumn? The ones which keep their leaves are called *evergreens*. Are yours *evergreens* or are they *deciduous* trees, the ones which lose their leaves:

Can you name any of the flowers (remember that even weeds like dandelions are flowers):

Are there any vegetables growing in the garden, in the allotment, or in the neighbours garden. What are they:

Do you know the names of any of the birds that you see in your garden, or in the park (what about the bird with the little red breast that stays behind in the winter, do you ever see him in your garden or in the park?):

What is your favourite flower?

Do you live in a county? If you do what is the county town? If you live in a metropolitan county what is its centre:

What is the main historical feature near your home? Is it a castle? A large house? A church? Or an archaeological site:

Which is your nearest river:

Which is your nearest airport:

Which is your nearest railway station:

Which is your nearest motorway:

How far do you think you live from the sea if
you travelled in a straight line to the nearest
stretch of coast (no point in Great Britain is
more than 1 1 7 kilometres from the sea):

Which is your nearest public library:

When is it open:

How many books can you borrow at one time:

What brand of petrol does your nearest filling
station sell:

Which dairy delivers your milk in the mornings:

Which is your nearest supermarket:

How many other supermarket chains can you name:

If you wanted to buy some medicine or some cough sweets, to which shop would you go:

Which is the ITV channel that you receive on your television most clearly:

If you wanted a game of tennis, where would you go:

Where is your nearest swimming-pool? Can you swim there in the winter:

Which newspapers are delivered to your home? If none are delivered, which do your family read during the week:

24

What's the name of your local church? If it's named after a saint, as many churches are, do you know why he or she became famous, or which group of people they are patron saint to:

Where is your nearest hospital:

Where is your nearest fire station:

Where is your nearest police station:

What number must you dial on the telephone to call any of these three emergency services:

YOUR SCHOOL

When was your school founded:

Why was your school given its name:

How many pupils are there:

How many teachers are there:

26

Can you give the names of two other schools like yours in the area (perhaps the ones you have sports fixtures against):

Does your headmaster or headmistress have any initials after his or her name? Do you know what they stand for:

How many terms have you been at your school:

How many terms have you got left:

What is the name of the school that you will be going to next? What sort of school is it:

Do you know what the initials C.S.E. and G.C.E. stand for (they're connected with examinations):

If you want to go to university or college after school you will probably need to pass some A-level exams. What does A-level mean:

YOU AND YOUR BODY

YOUR BODY AS A WHOLE

The optic nerve runs from your brain to two
organs of your body, which ones:

Your heart is the organ which pumps blood round your body, which parts of your body do you use for breathing:

The femur is the longest bone in your body, where is it:

Molars, incisors and canines are usually grouped together as a five-letter word beinning with 'T'. What is that word and where in your body do you find these three types of t----:

When all the bones in the human body are put together what is the whole framework called:

How many months is a baby in his or her mother's womb before he or she is born:

The word *digit* can mean any number from 0 to 9, but it also refers to two sets of parts of your body. Do you know which ones (there aren't that many *sets* to choose from and if you think of different ways of counting numbers you ought to come up with the answer):

Roughly how tall was the tallest
known human being:

Where in your body is the largest
muscle (it's near one of your limbs):

If part of someone's body is
paralysed, what is the matter with it:

Your body is made up of millions of tiny units
which can only be seen if they are examined
under a microscope. What are these units
called:

How tall are you?

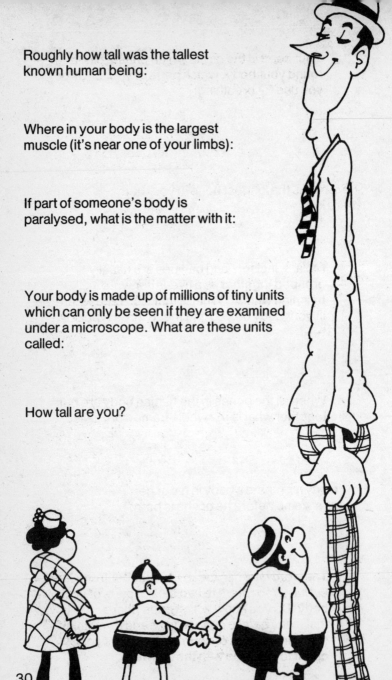

DEM BONES, DEM BONES, DEM DRY BONES

Fully grown adults and new born babies have different numbers of bones in their bodies. On average one has 350 bones and the other has 206. Which has which:

Your bones aren't dry of course, they're filled with a yellow substance. Do you know what it is (dogs are sometimes given m----- bones to chew):

Whereabouts in your body would you find your spine:

Where in your body is your pelvis:

There is one tiny bone in your body called the stirrup bone, which measures under 3.5 mm long. It is an important part of one of your senses. Where in your body is it:

The point at which your bones meet is called a joint. There are lots of joints all over your body. How many can you name:

What has happened to you if you suffer a fracture:

BLOOD,
BLOOD,
GLORIOUS BLOOD

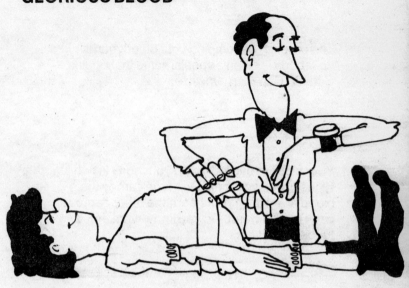

If a doctor or a nurse puts their fingers on the
inside of your wrist and then counts carefully
while they are looking at a watch they are
measuring something in your body. What is it?

Your blood is made up of a liquid called plasma
and three solids. One of these solids is called
the platelets and the other two are cells. But
each cell is given a colour. Do you know what
colours they are:

How much blood does the average man have
in his body?

The process of pumping your blood round
your body is given a special name that begins
with 'C'. Can you name it:

Your blood is carried round your body in two
types of elastic tubes. One type carries the
blood away from your heart, the other carries it
back to your heart. Do you know what these
tubes are called:

What important gas is absorbed into your
blood stream from the air that is breathed into
your lungs:

Do you know the name of the gas that is taken
out of your blood in your lungs (this gas has
two words in its name the last word is -*dioxide*)

34

YOUR ORGANS AND WHAT THEY HAVE TO DO

One of these isn't in fact an organ, which is it: heart; liver, kidney, eye:

In which of your organs would you find the retina, the iris and the pupil:

Why have you got a nose:

Can you name the organ in which you would find the left and right ventricles and the left and right atriums (obviously you'll have to go for *one* organ which is divided into two parts), which is it:

In two of the organs in our bodies we have the mechanism that helps us keep our balance. These organs both do the same job, but they have another separate function as well. Which organs are they:

Doctors have been able to develop a technique of transplanting human organs from a donor to a patient. How many organs can you think of which have been transplanted:

When you hold a seashell to your ear you hear a noise which a lot of people think is the sound of the sea. It isn't the sea of course, but what makes the noise (it comes from inside the ear itself):

What do your kidneys do:

DOWN THE HATCH — EATING AND DIGESTION

The energy produced by food is measured by a unit that begins with 'C'. You often hear about people counting these units when they are on diets. What's the unit called:

Which is longer the small intestine in your body or the large intestine:

Can you think of another name for dentures:

How many of the elements that we find in the food we eat, which we need to stay alive, can you name (salts, water and vitamins are three, what about the others?):

Whereabouts in your body is your saliva (it's part of your digestive process and it comes near the beginning of the process):

Where in your body is your food stored while it is slowly released into your digestive system:

What is your favourite day's menu:

BREAKFAST

LUNCH

TEA

SUPPER

How much do you weigh:

38

THINKING AND YOUR SENSES

Your body is criss-crossed with tiny thread-like organs which carry messages to and from your brain. Do you know what these are called:

What is measured in the units called decibels (it's something that affects one of your senses and the last part of the word **decibels** gives you a clue):

How many senses have you got and what are
they:

Who has the best hearing; a baby, a teenager,
or a man aged fifty:

Where in your mouth are your taste buds:

If you have trouble with your eyesight, which
specialist will provide you with glasses (your
doctor might tell you to have your eyes tested
for glasses, but he won't actually provide you
with the glasses):

Which person is reckoned to be more
intelligent, the one with an I.Q. of 50 or the one
with an I.Q. of 150:

HUMAN BEHAVIOUR

Why is it good for you to eat oranges (what important vitamin do they contain?):

What is the matter with you if you suffer from claustrophobia:

Roughly how many hours sleep each night does the average person need:

CHECK UPS AND MEDICAL TREATMENT

What instrument does a doctor use when he or she takes your temperature:

What does an anaesthetic do:

What's the common name for influenza:

What would need to be wrong with you for you to take an aspirin:

How many of the common illnesses which most people get when they are children have you had:

How regularly should you have your teeth examined by a dentist:

Which inoculations have you had (you might need to ask your Mum about the ones you had when you were very young):

How many well known diseases can you write down, (diseases of any sort will do):

Why is it important to bathe and disinfect any cut or graze you get:

Use this page to draw a picture of your body and then mark on it these parts: the spinal cord; the lungs; the nasal passage; the skull; the stomach; and the brain.

THE WORLD AT LARGE

WORLD WIDE

In which country do the Maoris live:

There is one country on Earth that fills an entire
continent. Can you think which one it is:

What is the name given to the half of the world
that lies north of the equator:

Which is there more of on Earth, land or sea:

How many days does it take the Earth to make
one complete circuit round the sun (this is the
same number of days of one of our units for
measuring time):

Which national flag carries a red maple leaf in
its centre:

Draw the flag of Japan in this space (colour in
the right colours if you can):

What is the money that is used in France:

The countries that produce oil have been in
the world news a lot in recent years. How
many of them can you name (many of them are
in the Middle East, but there are others in
America and Europe):

SKY HIGH — THE WORLD'S MOUNTAINS

What do we call mountains that sometimes explode blowing ash, rocks and molten lava into the air (Mt. St. Helens in the U.S.A. was one of these):

There can't be many people who don't know that Mt. Everest is the world's highest mountain. But do you know the names of the two countries on whose border Mt. Everest lies:

There is a famous mountain in Africa which lies almost on the equator. It is the second highest mountain in Africa and it is named after the country in which it stands. What's its name:

Mt. McKinley is the highest mountain in one of the continents. Which continent is it:

Mont Blanc, the Matterhorn and the Monte Rosa are all mountains in one European mountain range, which one:

Another mountain range in Europe, the Pyrennees, divides two countries. Can you name them:

Which is the highest mountain in Great Britain and where is it:

Do you know the highest point reached by any human being without the help of breathing equipment (most aircraft these days are fitted with breathing equipment although the passengers don't have to wear it strapped to their backs. There's no need to give the answer in metres, just name the place):

WATER, WATER EVERYWHERE
SEAS AND OCEANS

Which two oceans are joined by the Panama
Canal:

How many seas can you name. Here some to
start you off: The North Sea, the Baltic Sea,
the Sea of Japan. . .now you list as many
others as you can:

Which ocean pounds against shore of
Morocco in West Africa:

In which ocean does the island of
Madagascar, off the east coast of Africa, lie:

How many countries can you name with
coasts on the Mediterranean Sea:

Which ocean would you have to cross if you
wanted to sail directly from New Zealand to
Chile:

Which is the largest ocean in the world?

What movements of the oceans and seas are
caused by the pull of the Moon? You can see
this effect on the beach twice a day:

FROM AMAZON TO ZAIRE —
THE WORLD'S RIVERS

Although most people agree that the Amazon
is only the second longest river in the world,
there are still many who think that it is the
longest. Which is the other great river which is
the cause of this disagreement:

Which European river flows down the frontier
between France and Germany:

Make a list of all the rivers that you can name in
the U.S.A.:

Do you know what the river Zaire was called
before it was given its present name (the
former name was the same as that of a country
in the area):

The river Ganges is a great Asian river.
Through which country does it flow:

Between which two countries lie the Niagara
Falls:

Is the Orinoco in North or South America:

Which English river flows through these cities;
Oxford, Reading and London:

UNITED NATIONS — THE WORLD'S COUNTRIES

What is the main national language spoken in Mexico:

Its present name is Zimbabwe, but what did it used to be called:

Which important international organization has
its headquarters in a skyscraper in New York
City:

The flag of the Red Cross Organization is the
exact reverse of the flag of one European
country. Which country is it (the headquarters
of the Red Cross in Geneva might give you a
clue):

Do you know the name of the country that lies
between Afghanistan and India (this country
was once part of India, but it became
independent in 1947):

Alaska is in the north-west corner of North
America. It borders on Canada, but it doesn't
belong to Canada. Which country does own it:

Name all the countries you have visited
including the one you live in:

EUROPE

In which European city does the EEC have its headquarters (this city is the capital city of one European country):

Can you give another name for the Republic of Ireland:

Can you name one European country which used to be part of what the Romans called Gaul:

The Vatican is the smallest independent country in the world. In fact it is so small that it is actually inside an Italian city. Do you know the name of the city:

Do you know the capital cities of these European countries:

Denmark   —

Spain   —

East Germany   —

Italy   —

Poland   —

Norway   —

Which is the island that lies off the south coast of England opposite Southampton Water (mind how you spell it):

What are these regions of France famous for: Bordeaux; Burgundy; Champagne; and Alsace:

ASIA

Can you name any other Asian countries in which Arabic is the main language apart from Saudi Arabia:

This island lies to the south of India and it used to be called Ceylon. What's its name now:

What is a monsoon:

The country with the largest population in the world is in Asia. Do you know which country it is:

What is Taiwan: an Asian religion, a city in Japan, an island off the coast of China or a type of tree found in India:

Tokyo, Osaka, Nagoya and Hiroshima are all cities in which Asian country:

In which part of Asia is Mongolia; in the north; in the east; in the west; in the south; or in the centre:

One Asian country has a Great Wall named after it. Where is the Great Wall of. . . :

The Bering Strait separates Asia from another continent. Do you know which one:

AMERICA

Which is the largest country in South America:

Is Alberta part of the U.S.A. or part of Canada:

One of these cities is not in North America,
which is it: Chicago; Los Angeles;
Philadelphia; Boston; Sydney; Detroit;
Vancouver; Montreal:

Which is the very long, thin country that runs
down the west coast of South America:

In which U.S. state is the city of Dallas:

The Statue of Liberty stands on an island at the
entrance to one great western port. Do you
know which port it is:

Can you write down the name of
five states in the U.S.A. (if you can,
try and write down
some more as well).
There are 50 of them in all:

What is the capital of
the U.S.A.:

AFRICA

Whereabouts in Africa is the Cape of Good Hope:

What is the name of the great desert that stretches across much of North Africa:

In which country in Africa can you see the
pyramids:

Which African country lies across the sea from
the rock of Gibraltar:

The Boer War was fought in Africa at the very
beginning of the twentieth century, but do you
know in which country it was fought:

Algiers and Tunis are the capital cities of which
two African countries:

Three African countries have names that begin
with 'Z'. What are they:

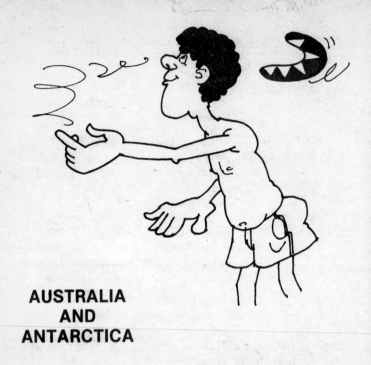

AUSTRALIA
AND
ANTARCTICA

What's the name of the island that lies to the south of the south-east corner of Australia:

Which of these Australian cities is the capital of Australia: Melbourne; Adelaide; Perth; Sydney; Canberra:

Is the South Pole higher above sea level, or lower than the North Pole:

Which of these animals will you not find in
Antarctica: polar bears; penguins; and
reindeer:

What is the name of the famous throwing stick,
used by aborigines in Australia, which flies
back to its thrower:

How many animals can you name which are
native to Australia:

Which country is nearest to Australia: Papua
New Guinea; New Zealand; or the Philippines:

Can you name two of the six states of
Australia:

Does the Great Barrier Reef lie on the south-
west, north-east or north-west coast of
Australia:

FAMOUS SITES OF THE WORLD

In which country is the
Taj Mahal:

What famous site does
every visitor to the
Italian city of Pisa
want to see:

What famous construction
did Gustave Eiffel erect in
Paris between 1887
and 1889:

How many of the Seven
Wonders of the
ancient world can you
name:

PEOPLE, PLACES AND EVENTS

KINGS

How many English kings have there been named Charles:

Which European countries have kings on the throne at present (kings mind, not **queens**):

King John was made to sign a famous document in 1215. What was that document called (its name has two words, the last word begins with 'C'):

Which English king commanded the compiling of the Domesday Book in the eleventh century:

In a very well known Christmas carol, the city of Bethlehem is named after one of the kings of Israel. Can you remember which king that is:

One English king named George was king during the First World War and another king named George was king during the Second World War. Which King Georges were they, and what relations were they to our Queen:

FIRST WORLD WAR   **SECOND WORLD WAR**

He wasn't very good when it came to baking cakes, but he was a just and powerful king of Wessex. Who was he:

Can you think of the name of the most famous horror film monster shaped like a giant gorilla (his name begins with two 'K's):

Which British king lived at Camelot and ate his meals at a huge round table:

Which 'Good King. . .' went out into the snow on St. Stephen's Day to take food and fuel to a poor countryman of his:

How many English kings have been named Edward and can you remember when the last one came to the throne, although he was never crowned king. (You don't **have** to know the year, '1920's'; '1870's; or whichever decade it was, will do):

Which English king defeated the Norsemen at the battle of Stamford Bridge and in the same year was shot in the eye at the Battle of Hastings:

QUEENS

Write down the names of as many queens of England that you can think of, without looking any up:

Who was the Scottish queen beheaded during the reign of Queen Elizabeth I:

Who was married to the second Queen Mary:

What is the Queen Mother's christian name:

Queen Mary, Queen Elizabeth and **QE II** are
all what, beside being the names of queens

Several European countries have queens on
the throne at present. Which countries are
they:

Who was married to Queen Guinevere:

Which famous Egyptian queen is said to have
killed herself with a poisonous snake called an
asp:

Which famous Briton queen revolted against
the Romans in AD61. She was Queen of the
Iceni tribe and her name began with a B:

EMPERORS AND EMPIRES

What is the name given to the group of
countries which used belong to the old British
Empire:

Do you know what the adjective is that
describes things connected with an empire or
its rulers (the adjective which does this for
kings or queens is **royal**):

This emperor was forced to leave his empire in January 1979. He then lived in Egypt and Central America before he died a short time after. His empire was in the Middle East and he was replaced by a religious leader known as an ayatollah. Who was the emperor:

Who was the French emperor who was defeated by the English and the Prussians at the Battle of Waterloo in 1815:

How was the Roman empire governed before it became an empire? Was it a monarchy or a republic:

How many empires in history can you name (you've been given the British and Roman empires already, how many more can you add?):

PALACES, CASTLES AND CHURCHES

Can you think which is the largest inhabited castle in the world (it's in southern England):

In which famous cathedral were the Prince and Princess of Wales married in 1981:

St. Thomas Becket was martyred there in 1170. The church is in southern England somewhere. Do you know where:

I'm sure you know that the Queen lives in Buckingham Palace, but how many other palaces can you name in Great Britain:

What was the **keep** in many old castles and what was the moat:

KEEP   **MOAT**

What is the connection between the Princes of Wales and Caernarfon Castle:

BATTLES

One English king named Henry commanded
the English army at the battle of Agincourt in
1415. Which King Henry was he;

A famous air battle took place in 1940
between the German Luftwaffe and the
R.A.F. . Do you now what this is called:

Make a list of all the battles that have been
fought on British soil that you can think of. (The
last of these was the Battle of Culloden Moor
which was fought in 1746):

WARS

Britain fought the **Opium War** against one country in Asia during the middle of the nineteenth century. Which country was that:

Which war ended on the eleventh hour of the eleventh day of the eleventh month of 1918:

What happened at the Hawaiian port named Pearl Harbour on Sunday 7 December, 1941:

In America this war is called **The American Revolution**. What is it called in Great Britain:

How many countries can you name that were invaded by Germany during the Second World War:

Between 1455 and 1485 the two powerful houses of York and Lancaster were fighting each other to win control of the throne of England. These wars were named after two different coloured flowers of the same species. Do you know what the flower was, and which house had which colour:

FLOWER   LANCASTER   YORK

Which twentieth century war came to end with the fall of the city of Saigon, th capital of one country in Asia:

During the American Civil War the Confederates fought against the Unionists. Which side won:

During which century was the Spanish Civil War fought:

ANCIENT TIMES

What were the great pyramids of ancient
Egypt used for:

What nationality was the great military leader
named Alexander the Great:

Who was the Roman general who commanded the first Roman invasion of Britain:

Who led the Children of Israel to freedom from Egypt:

Which African animals did the Carthaginian general named Hannibal lead over the Alps into Italy (these animals were used by his armies in battle):

Do you know the name of city in Asia Minor where the Greeks fought for ten years before they finally captured it by using a gigantic wooden horse:

Which ancient peoples dressed in the garment known as a **toga**:

EXPLORERS AND DISCOVERIES

Which continent was explored by the Scottish missionary David Livingstone:

Which country was Christopher Columbus *hoping to find* when he set sail across the Atlantic in 1492:

Who was the first European to command a voyage all the way round the world (he was an Englishman):

How many countries can you name that were visited by Captain Cook:

Who was the first Englishman to lead a party to reach the South Pole (he died on his return from it):

What nationality was the explorer and traveller named Marco Polo who made an historic journey to China in the thirteenth century:

Which Europeans were the first to discover America:

OOPS!

CELEBRITY ROLL-CALL

Why is the name of Sir Christopher Wren
famous:

Who was the French peasant girl who inspired
the French to defeat the English in the fifteenth
century and who was later burned at the stake
(she was made a saint in 1920):

What nationality was the painter Vincent Van
Gogh:

WORKS OF GENIUS

Why is Wolfgang Amadeus Mozart so well known:

Which great Italian painter painted the *Mona Lisa*:

Make a list of all the British playwrights you can think of:

One of these is not a composer: Brahms; Beethoven; Picasso; Sibelius. Which is the odd one out:

NATURAL WORLD

YOUR OWN NOAH'S ARK —
THE WHOLE ANIMAL KINGDOM

Imagine that it is a warm summer's night.
Imagine that you are walking silently into a
wood. Imagine yourself sitting down under a
large oak tree in the middle of the wood.
Imagine that you sit here for a couple of hours
listening to the life in the wood all around you.
Sometimes you catch a sight of an animal, a
bird, or an insect in the bright moonbeams that
shine through the branches. You've taken a
notebook and a pencil with you so make a list
of all the creatures that you might see and hear
in this wood:

Do you know which is the largest creature ever
known to have lived:

What exactly do we mean when we describe a
species of animal as being **extinct**:

How many animals can you think of which produce milk:

What are hibernating animals doing while they are hibernating:

This animal is believed to have looked like a horse — with one very big difference. From its forehead a long, straight horn sticks out to the front. Can you remember what this mythical animal is called:

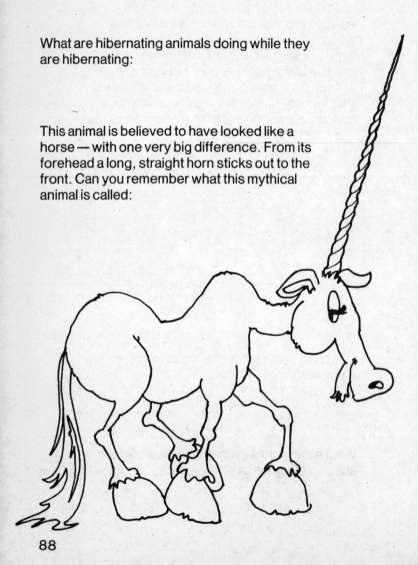

DOMESTIC ANIMALS — AT HOME AND ON THE FARM

What is the name of the animal that gives birth to lambs:

Young dogs are called puppies, young cats are called kittens, what are young goats called (children are often given the same name):

Which pets are kept in cages or hutches:

From which animal do we get pork and bacon:

How many farmyard animals can you name:

What type of animal is a saluki (is it a type of cat; a type of dog; a type of horse; or another type of animal?):

How many breeds of dogs and cats can you name:

DOGS   **CATS**

SEA CREATURES — LIFE BENEATH THE WAVES

How many arms does an octopus have:

There are lots of sea creatures that live in shells. These are called shellfish. Some of them move about the sea bed and others stick themselves to rocks. How many shellfish can you think of:

Do you know why whales, dolphins and porpoises are **not** fish:

UP IN THE AIR —
THE WORLD OF BIRDS

What do birds do when they **migrate**:

There's one bird which is so lazy that it can't be bothered to build its own nest or even hatch its own eggs. This bird lays its eggs in other birds' nests and gets them to do the hard work for it. Do you know which bird this is:

Which is the fastest **running** bird in the world (it's one of the few birds that **can't** fly):

What do we mean when we describe birds as **birds of prey** and how many birds of prey can you name:

ON ALL FOURS —
FOUR-LEGGED ANIMALS

This animal looks similar to a horse but its body is covered with stripes. What's its name:

The lion is the king of the animal world and he's also a member of the cat family. Which other animals that you can think of belong to the same family (you can only count one pet in your list!)

There are two principal types of elephant found on earth. One is the African elephant. What's the other one called:

A fawn is young animal that lives in woods or forests. What will it be when it grows up and becomes a fully grown animal:

Chi Chi and An An are both very rare animals. They belong to the same species which is only found now in remote parts of China. There's an Italian car named after this species. Can you think what sort of animals Chi Chi and An An are:

Which large white bear lives in the Arctic:

Herbivores are plant-eaters. Do you know the correct name for meat-eaters — it begins with a C:

Which four-legged desert animal stores fat in its humps:

Is the horn of a rhinoceros made of bone, ivory or hair:

SPORTING ANIMALS

What type of birds are used in long-distance flying races:

Races between dogs that belong to a very fast breed are very popular now. These dogs chase an electric hare around a circuit and the spectators place bets on the dogs that they think will win. Do you know the name of these racing dogs:

In the Middle Ages hunters used trained birds to catch their prey. These birds used to wear hoods over their heads until the hunter released them to fly after their victims. What sort of birds were used for this form of hunting:

There is a special breed of dog used in fox hunting. Do you know what that breed is:

Which of these famous horse races takes place over jumps — the *Grand National* or the *Derby*:

Can you name a country in which you might expect to see a camel race:

Which animal competes in a Dressage event:

Uprights, parallels and spreads are used in which sporting event:

CREEPY CRAWLIES — INSECTS, SPIDERS AND BUGS

We only eat one type of food that is directly produced by an insect. This is a sweet tasting food. Can you think what it is and which insect makes it:

If an animal scratches itself a lot the chances are that it is being bitten by a small blood feeding insect. These tiny insects sometimes bite human beings too. Do you know what they are called:

Do you know what sort of creature a Red
Admiral is (its name should give you a clue):

Tarantulas and Black Widows both belong to
the same animal group. Do you know what sort
of creatures they are:

These creatures catch their food in special
nets that they spin themselves. What are they
called:

How many legs does a spider have:

How many butterflies can you name:

Which tropical insect carries the disease
called malaria:

What sort of insect is a bluebottle:

ANIMAL HEROS
AND STARS

Who is the flying dog that took on the Red
Baron single-handed:

Who is believed to have ridden from London to
York non-stop on his horse named Black
Bess:

Do you know what type of dog the T.V. star
Lassie is:

Snowy is a small, white dog who accompanies
his young master on all sorts of adventures.
Who is Snowy's master:

Who rode the Wild West on a horse named
Silver:

There is a well known Sherlock Holmes story
which is centred round a wild, savage animal.
The story is called The ----- of the Baskervilles.
Do you know the missing word:

How many of Beatrix Potter's animal stories
can you name:

There are many types of shark living in the sea.
Very few of them are dangerous to humans.
But there is one shark, the star of the film
Jaws, which is known to have attacked
people. This shark is known by a colour and its
name begins with the work 'Great'. Can you
complete its name:

ANIMALS THAT HAVE COME AND GONE

Do you know the name of the type of prehistoric elephant which used to roam the earth. Some of these were covered with thick, shaggy coats to keep out the cold. And the animal has the same name as an adjective which means 'huge':

Tyrannosaurus Rex was the largest two-legged member of its animal family that ever lived. Many of the other members of the family like **Diplodocus** moved around on four legs. This animal family is the best known group of prehistoric animals. Do you know which it is:

The sabre-toothed tiger was a fierce, meat-eating animal which lived in prehistoric times. It gets its name from the two long teeth which stuck down from its upper jaw. But do you know what a **sabre** really is:

ANIMALS AND THEIR HOMES

What would you expect to find living in an
aquarium:

What sorts of creatures are kept in an aviary:

This fish lives in both fresh water and salt
water. It often swims thousands of kilometres
back to the river or stream where it was born to
lay its own eggs. Which fish is it:

How many birds can you think of which make
their nests on the ground and not in trees:

What is a rabbit's home called:

Where do bees live:

This reptile carries its home round on its back.
What is it:

Which woodland animal lives in a sett. It has a
black and white striped head:

Baby kangaroos and wallabies have a special
'home'. Do you know what it is:

This animal has four legs. They say that it never forgets. This animal drinks through its mouth although it looks as if it drinks through part of its nose. This animal is found on two continents, but the ears of one type are different from the ears of the other. Can you draw a picture of this animal on this page:

SCIENCE,
TECHNOLOGY
AND SPACE

GENERAL SCIENCE

Where does a scientist normally do his work:

What is an abacus used for:

What do the abbreviations **km/h** and **m.p.h.** stand for:

What would you use a protractor for measuring:

So far 107 elements have been detected.
These elements make up all the known matter
in the universe. Some of these elements are
gases, some are liquids and the majority of
them are solids. Many of the elements are
metals like gold and copper. How many other
metal elements can you think of:

Can you think of another name for nuclear
energy:

How many lines are there on the normal
television screen:

What important invention was made by
Alexander Graham Bell (the world has been
ringing with his invention ever since!):

How many fuels like wood and petrol can you
think of:

SCIENCES AND SCIENTISTS

What is the scientific name for the study of living things:

What does a meteorologist study. (He or she doesn't study meteors, as you might think, but meteorologists do spend a long time studying the sky. Why?):

What is geology:

What part of the human body is the principal study of the psychologist:

Why would you expect to find an archaeologist spending a lot of time digging:

Which sciences can you think of that are taught in schools (here's one to get you started — mathematics):

What do bacteriologists study:

For which branch of study is Albert Einstein remembered:

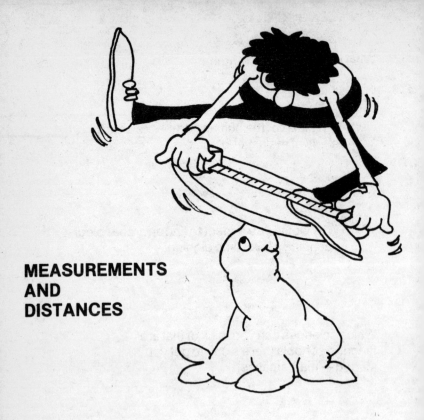

MEASUREMENTS
AND
DISTANCES

Can you think of an animal which is measured in **hands**:

What are the two scales commonly used for measuring temperatures:

What is measured in **fathoms**:

How many sides are there in a **pentagon**:

What is the **diameter** of a circle:

In what sort of race would you hear the
commentator referring to distances in
furlongs:

How many metres are there in three and a half
kilometres:

Can you think of one of the units used in
measuring electricity:

In which book would you expect to find
distances measured in **cubits**:

TIME

How does a sundial help you tell the time:

Two of the months in our calender are named after Roman statesmen. One was a famous general, the other was the first Roman emperor. Can you think which months these are:

What is the usual name given to a period of one
hundred years:

Do you know what the initials G.M.T. stand for:

Today wristwatches work by clockwork
mechanisms or by a more modern way. What
are these modern watches generally called?
(Their name begins with a 'Q'):

How many minutes are there in a seven-day
week:

If the time is noon in London will it be seven
o'clock in the morning in New York, or five
o'clock in the afternoon:

GREAT INVENTIONS AND INVENTORS

In 1955 a British inventor named Sir
Christopher Cockerell invented a totally new
type of vehicle which can travel over water as
well as over land. This vehicle floats on a
cushion of air. What is it called:

What method of sending signals was
developed by an American named Samuel
Morse in 1837. His invention still bears his
name. What is it called and what does it consist
of:

What did the two Hungarian brothers named
Lazlo and Georg Biro invent in 1938. (You
might even be holding one at the moment
without realizing the connection):

As early as 1589 Sir John Harrington invented
a water-closet, or W.C. . What's another name
for his invention:

In 1590 a Dutch inventor named Zacharius Janssen developed an instrument which magnified tiny objects until human beings could see them. Today you find instruments like his first one in most scientific laboratories. What did he invent:

This inventor's name has become associated with tyres and other products made from rubber ever since he invented pneumatic bicycle tyres (ones filled with air) in 1888. Do you know what his surname was:

HEAVENS ABOVE —
THE UNIVERSE

What's the more common name given to
meteors:

What do we call it when the moon gets
between the sun and the Earth and blocks out
the sunlight for a short time (the word begins
with an 'e' and ends with an 'e'):

How many of the planets can you name (there
are nine if you include the Earth):

The Earth circles round the sun but what
circles round the Earth:

Which of these studies the positions of the
stars and uses his or her findings to predict
what will happen to any one of us in the future
— an astronomer or an astrologer:

Is the gravity on the surface of the moon
stronger or weaker than gravity on Earth:

What is the Milky Way (no — it's not the
chocolate bar):

One of the planets is surrounded by rings.
Which planet is that:

Which is the 'dark side' of the moon:

What is the 'orbit' of a satellite:

What is the name of the scientific study of the sun, the moon, the planets and the stars:

To which of the heavenly bodies does the adjective 'lunar' apply:

Until Copernicus taught that the earth moved round the sun, in the middle of the sixteenth century, what had people believed to be the case:

What is the name of the world's first reusable spacecraft:

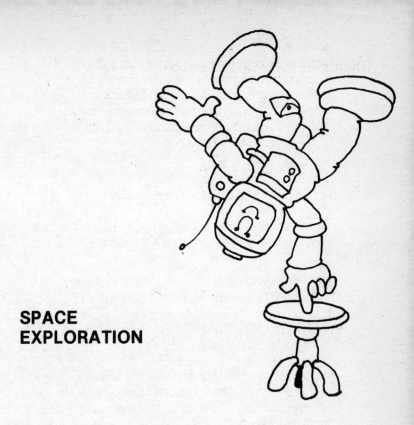

SPACE
EXPLORATION

Why do astronauts experience
weightlessness in space:

Which country was the first to put a man in
space, the U.S.S.R. or the U.S.A.:

Who was the first man to step on to the surface
of the moon — Neil Armstrong; Buz Aldrin; or
Michael Collins:

The Russians have an orbiting space station
which is called *Salyut* and the Americans had
an orbiting space station until it fell back to
earth in 1979. Can you remember what the
American space station was called:

Why is the name of Yuri Gagarin remembered
today:

Are there astronauts travelling in the *Voyager I*
that has so far visited Jupiter and Saturn:

The Apollo programme was the one which
landed a man on the moon, but do you know
the names of any of the other missions that
came before Apollo:

Can you remember the name of the vehicle
which some American moon missions used for
travelling over the surface of the moon:

Are American spacecraft launched from
Houston in Texas or from Cape Kennedy in
Florida:

Use this page to draw your own picture of the
American Space Shuttle on its launching pad.
(But before you start, think why the Space
Shuttle looks different on the launching to the
way it looks when it comes into land at the end
of a mission. Does that give you a clue?):

TRANSPORT AND TRAVEL

ON THE MOVE —
TRAVEL IN GENERAL

Every year there is a famous cycling race round the largest country in Europe. Top cyclists from all over the world take part in this race which lasts about three weeks. Do you know what this race is called:

Do you know what a rickshaw is:

Radar was invented in 1922. It is used for navigation. Can you think which types of vehicles are fitted with radar:

What would you expect to find inside a **hangar**:

Sailors use charts for finding their way at sea. What is the name for the 'charts' which land travellers use:

What was the *Cutty Sark*: a famous ship; a famous locomotive; a famous racing car; or a famous aircraft:

How many makes of motor bike can you list:

Right and left are given two different names in ships and aircraft when you are looking towards the bow of the ship or the front of the aircraft. What are those names:

RIGHT

LEFT

AIRCRAFT

Who were the first men to fly a heavier than air machine successfully:

Graf von Zeppelin invented a new type of flying machine in 1900. These aircraft were popular during the first thirty years of this century, but after several serious accidents they were no longer used. More modern ones are making a come-back today. Many of the earliest bore von Zeppelin's name, but what was the more general name for his invention:

Which was the world's first supersonic airliner (it's still in use):

When a pilot talks about altitude what is he or she referring to:

Many historic aircraft flew during the Second World War. Can you name any of them:

Before the invention of the jet engine what was the usual way of moving an aircraft through the air:

What is the nickname given to the large jet airliner known as the Boeing 747:

How many airports in the British Isles can you name:

The largest British airline is British Airways. How many foreign airlines can you think of:

There are two ways of applying the brakes in a car. What are they:

Henry Ford was the founder of the Ford Motor Company, one of the world's largest manufacturers of motor vehicles. Do you know what nationality Henry Ford was:

In America most cars run on gasoline. In England cars run on the same fuel, but we call it something else. What:

What does the speedometer in a car's dashboard tell you:

127

In which country are these makes of car
produced: Datsun; Toyota; Honda; Subaru;
and Colt:

All cars have electrical systems. When the
engines are running electricity is generated in
either alternators or dynamos. But where in a
car is electricity stored:

Which European car manufacturer builds the
Metro:

Which part of a car's engine keeps it cool (it's
at the front of the engine and it's name begins
with an 'R'):

What is special about **convertible** cars;

On which side of the road do they drive in the
U.S.A. (think of any American programmes
which you have seen on television — that
should give you a clue):

In which country are Fiat cars made:

What colour are the brake, or stop lights on a car:

If you are driving down a British road at night your headlights will be reflected by hundreds of studs in the centre of the road. What are these reflecting studs called:

What is the name given to the cars which you can drive without having to change the gear yourself:

Can you think of the name of the most luxurious and expensive British car which is manufactured by a company that also makes aircraft and other engines:

What car would you most like to own one day:

SHIPS
AND
BOATS

What do you use for moving a canoe through the water:

What navigational instrument does a sailor use to find his way at sea:

Whereabouts in a ship is her hold:

Can you think of the name of Nelson's flagship at the battle of Trafalgar (it was the ship on which he was killed and you can see the ship preserved today at Portsmouth):

What is the name for ships that can sail under
the sea:

What part of a sailing dinghy holds up the sail:

There have been several ways of sending
signals at sea throughout the centuries. The
most modern way is the use of radio signals.
But what other methods of signalling can you
think of:

Which group of people used to hunt and travel
in kayaks:

What is the name given to the ships that sail
across the English Channel carrying
passengers and motor vehicles. These ships
are generally called cross-Channel -------.
What's the missing word:

How many cruise liners can you name (some
are named after members of the royal family):

131

TRAINS AND RAILWAYS

Before the introduction of modern railway engines, which are powered by diesel-electric motors, how were railway engines powered. (These old-fashioned engines are sometimes called ------engines after the five-letter word which describes the source of their power). What is that five-letter word:

What do the points on a railway track do:

What happens in a railway signal-box:

Can you think of another name for the railway network that is sometimes called the **tube**:

Which well known bear got his name from a railway station:

The high-speed trains which have been used on inter-city routes for several years are sometimes known by a number. These are called --- trains. Do you know what this three-figure number is:

There are several famous main line railway stations in London. How many of these can you name:

If you are looking at a railway timetable and you see the symbol of a crossed knife and fork, what does that tell you about the train beside which the symbol appears:

Which member of a train's crew travels in the van at the rear of a train. This van is sometimes called the -----'- van:

FAMOUS JOURNEYS AND ROUTES

The ancient trade route which ran across
Central Asia from China to the west was
named after a type of material that was only
produced in China at that time. Do you know
what that route was called.

Long-distance walking has become popular in recent years. Today many people are able to explore remote parts of the British Isles by walking one of the many long-distance footpaths that have been established. One of the oldest and longest of these runs from Derbyshire north to the Scottish border. It runs along the backbone of northern England following a line of hills from which it gets its name. What is this footpath called:

Watling Street, the Fosse Way and Ermine Street were all ancient roads in Britain. Who built them:

Which motorway would you take if you wanted to drive west from London to Bristol:

Which motorway would you take if you wanted to drive north from London to Leeds:

There was a famous train which used to run between Paris and Istanbul. Do you remember what it was called (the train featured in an Agatha Christie story, which was later turned into a film of the same title):

HOLIDAYS AND DESTINATIONS

In which country is the popular holiday area
called the Costa del Sol:

Which English holiday resort is famous for its
tower, its lights and for the political
conferences that take place there each year.
(The name begins with 'B'):

Can you think of the European countries to
which you might travel for a skiing holiday:

List the
places you have
spent holidays
in over the last
five years:

Use this page to draw a picture of a car. Then draw in the following parts of the car in the places where you would expect to find them: the **bonnet**; the **exhaust pipe**; the **gearbox**; the **wing mirrors**; the **windscreen wipers**; the **petrol tank**; the **handbrake**; the **rear-axle**; the **shock absorbers**; the **speedometer**; and the **engine**.

Draw your family's car if you have one:

SPORTING WORLD

SPORTING LIFE — SPORTS IN GENERAL

What sport is played on the pitch at Twickenham:

Where does the Horse of the Year Show take place:

For which sport is the town of Cowes in the Isle of Wight famous:

Where were the last World Cup finals held:

Who was the last player to win the women's singles final at Wimbledon:

What is the name of the game which is like hockey, but which is played on horseback:

What is the name of the area of short grass that surrounds a hole on a golf-course:

Which sport do you associate with a three-day event:

Epées and sabres are both types of sword. In which sport are they used. (Its name begins with an 'F'):

Every spring a famous races takes place on the river Thames in London. Two crews race against each other from Putney Bridge to Mortlake. This race is one of the oldest rowing races in the world. In 1981 history was made when a girl took part in this race for the first time. Do you know what the race is called and who races who:

RACE   CREW   vs.   CREW

Do you know what is the correct name for **soccer**:

In which sport is a shuttlecock used instead of a ball:

The Americans call it football, but it uses a ball shaped like one which is used in a game in Great Britain and we usually call that game something else. Which is the British game that uses a ball that shape:

Do you know the name of the racing circuit where the British Grand Prix is held:

TEAM GAMES

How many players are there in a hockey side:

How many players are there in a rugby league
side:

How many players are there in a
netball side:

How many players are there in a
basketball side:

If you wanted to watch a
baseball game which would be
the best country to visit:

How many players are there
on the field during a cricket
match:

**WINTER
SPORTS**

In which country were the last winter Olympic
Games held:

Can you think of a skiing event in which
competitors ski without the aid of ski sticks:

In which winter sport do competitors take part
in slalom races:

What is the name of the object which ice-
hockey players hit across the ice in place of a
ball:

ATHLETICS

How many events make up a decathlon competition:

What is the name of the race in which teams of runners compete against each other with one runner in each team covering part of the total distance before he or she hands over to a team-mate:

144

Do you know what is the correct name for the kind of spear that is thrown in athletic competitions:

What is the name of the very long running race that covers over 42 kilometres and which is named after a battle that was fought in ancient Greece:

What is the name of the athletics event in which competitors try to throw a heavy weight as far as they can:

What is the name of the heavy disk that is also thrown in athletics events:

Can you name one of the world records that Sebastian Coe has broken:

SPORTS AROUND THE WORLD

In which country does the Sydney to Hobart
yacht race take place:

Do you know in which country the earliest
game of tennis originated:

In which country did judo originate:

Curling is similar to bowls except that it is played on ice with special 'stones' instead of bowls. Do you know in which country it originated:

There are several car rallies that take place every year. Can you name one of them and the country in which it takes place:

In which country would you expect to play **hurling**:

In which country did cricket originate:

Basketball and netball are closely related, but which sport was invented first, and in which country was each first played:

FAMOUS SPORTSMEN AND WOMEN

John Curry and Robin Cousins are both outstanding British performers in one winter sports' event. Which one is that:

What was Christine Lloyd's name before she married John Lloyd:

What nationality is the tennis star Bjorn Borg:

With which sport was Muhammad Ali associated:

Why is Mary Peters well known in the athletic world:

Sir Donald Bradman was a famous Australian sportsman. Which sport did he play:

Who was the England goal keeper when
England last won the World Cup:

Allan Wells won an event in the 1980 Olympic
Games. Do you remember which it was:

Can you think of one of the sports in which
Prince Philip has excelled (most of them are to
do with horses):

SPORTS CLUBS AND TEAMS AND
THEIR EMBLEMS

What is the full name of the football team
known as Spurs:

What do the initials M.C.C. stand for:

Which national rugby team are known as the
Springboks:

Which English football team has its home
ground at Anfield:

Which English football team has a day of the
week in its name:

Which two teams compete in the Wightman
Cup competition:

Where do the All Blacks come from:

What was the last emblem of the England
World Cup team:

Can you draw it:

SPORTS EQUIPMENT

In which sport would you use parallel bars:

In which sport would you use fences:

In which sport would you use hurdles:

What is the name for the types of sledge that are used in winter sports competitions with teams of four men:

Can you think of the sports in which saddles play an important part:

Which sports events are finished with a chequered flag:

In which table game do you use a cue:

In which sport do the players compete with clubs:

Which sports you can think of that take place inside a ring:

SPORTS PEOPLE AND THEIR ROLES

In which sport would you expect to find a 'silly mid-off':

What is the name of the man or woman who runs with the players and controls a game of football:

What is the name of the man or woman who
controls a tennis match:

In which sport do scullers take part:

In which sport do you see matadors and
picadors competing:

How many sports can you think of in which
there are goalkeepers:

MON's, KYU's and DAN's are all grades of
sports people in which sport:

In which sport would you expect to find a fly
half:

ABBREVIATIONS IN SPORT

Do you know to which football club these
initials refer W.B.A.:

What is the A.A.A.:

If you look on the side of a squash ball you will
usually see the initials S.R.A. . Do you know
what they refer to (if you know the full name of
the sport it will almost give you the answer):

In which sport do teams compete in the
U.E.F.A. Cup:

Which sport is controlled by the W.B.A.:

What does it mean if you are l.b.w.:

The I.L.T.F. controls one popular sport. Which
one is it:

Do you know what the initials W.T.T. refer to
when applied to the sport of lawn tennis:

SPORTS IN THE AIR

What is sky-diving:

Can you think of any country in the world
where you might be able to watch kite-fighting:

What is the name of the sport in which competitors are drawn into the air inside aircraft with long wings but no engines and they then drift about the sky using air-currents to keep them airborne:

This sport is sometimes called **hawking**, but can you think of its correct name:

What is the name of the sport in which competitors fire arrows through the air at circular targets:

Can you think of a way of describing hang-gliding:

LEISURE

FUN AND GAMES —
LEISURE IN GENERAL

Can you think of another game which is similar
to billiards:

What would you be attending if you went to the
Royal Festival Hall in London one evening:

How many pieces are there on a chess-board
at the start of a game:

What is the name of the city in which Batman
and Robin struggle to maintain law and order:

The Beatles were one of the most popular
groups in the 1960's. How many of the
Beatles can you name. (There were four of
them):

Today most discs are recorded in stereophonic sound which gives the impression that the sound is coming from more than one direction. What is the four-letter word that describes the way in which discs used to be recorded:

What's the name given to a type of play where most of the words are sung:

Who came from the planet Krypton:

AT THE MOVIES — FILMS AND THE CINEMA

What does it mean when a film is given a 'U' certificate:

Walt Disney is one of the most famous names in cartoon films. How many of his films or his cartoon characters can you name:

In which country in Europe is the film *The Sound of Music* set:

Which famous superhero was played on the cinema screen by the actor Christopher Reeve, who did a lot of flying in the part:

Do you know the name of the actor who played James Bond in the film *For Your Eyes Only*:

What was the full name of the 'ark' which was at the centre of adventure film *Raiders of the Lost Ark*:

Who was the evil count from Transylvania who turned into a vampire and sucked his victims' blood:

THE WORLD OF LITERATURE — BOOKS AND PLAYS

Do you know the name of the man who used to tell the stories about Brer Rabbit and Brer Fox:

Rudyard Kipling wrote a famous story about Mowgli and his animal friends. This story was later made into a cartoon film. Can you remember what it was called:

J.R.R. Tolkien has become famous for his stories set in the Shire, which deal with the adventures of curious little creatures. One of his books is simply called after one of these creatures. What name did Tolkien give to them:

How many of the characters created by Enid Blyton can you remember:

Jonathan Swift wrote a story about the
adventures of a man named Gulliver. Do you
know what his surname was:

Cecil Day Lewis wrote a number of children's
stories which have been popular for many
years. Can you name one of them:

Who was Robinson Crusoe's companion on
his desert island:

He wrote *David Copperfield; Oliver Twist* and *The Old Curiosity Shop* as well as many other books. What was his name:

In which famous play, which is often performed at Christmas, does the pirate Captain Hook appear:

William Shakespeare was a famous English playwright who lived from 1564 until 1616. How many of his plays can you name. (He wrote several about medieval kings of England, so that might give you a clue. And many of his others were named after individual people):

A SIGHT FOR SQUARE EYES —
THE WORLD OF TELEVISION

What is the name of Captain Kirk's starship:

Which well known doctor travels through time and space in the *Tardis*:

Do you know what is the alternative to monochrome television:

Who are the actors who play the parts of Sapphire and Steel in the television series of the same name:

Which television hero was first played by Roger Moore and is now played by the actor named Ian Ogilvy:

If you wanted to find out what was being broadcast on B.B.C. radio and television the following week which publication would you need to buy:

How many of the independent television networks can you name:

Blue Peter is named after a piece of equipment that is found on board a ship. Have you any idea what that piece of equipment is:

How many of Charlie's Angels can you name:

HOBBIES AND PASTIMES

What would you be doing if you had kitted
yourself out with strong boots, a rucksack, a
map and an anorak.

What hobby would you be following if you
were using a keep net, floats, and maggots:

Where would you go if you wanted to do some
brass rubbing:

What is another name for the craft of
woodwork:

In which hobby would you use pinking shears:

Who might you expect to keep their collection
in albums:

What do potholers do:

What do the initials Y.H.A. stand for:

For which hobby would you need a light metre
and possibly a dark-room:

Who uses an easel and a palette:

What might you be doing if you were drying
your work in a kiln:

Do you know what **papier-mâché** is:

Who might use an ice-axe and why might he or
she use it:

Can you think of another name for a
marionette:

Who would you expect to make use of an
allotment:

172

MUSIC AND MUSIC MAKING

Which country do you associate with the
music of the bagpipes:

The strings and the woodwind are two
sections of an orchestra. How many other
sections can you name:

The harpsichord is similar to a younger and more common instrument today. What instrument is that:

How is the sound produced in an organ:

Do you know in which country jazz music originated:

What do you usually need when you want to play the violin:

What sort of instrument is a mandoline:

Can you think of the names of any British composers or song writers:

Use this page to draw a picture of a sailing boat
and then mark on your picture the following
parts of the boat's equipment: the **rudder**; the
jib; the **mainsail**; the **boom**; the **mast**; the
centreboard; and the **tiller**:
What would you name the boat:

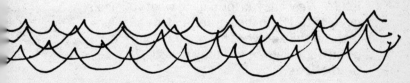

PREDICTIONS

This book started with questions about you and it's going to end with some more. But the first lot dealt with your past. The questions which follow here deal with your future.

How can I answer questions about something that hasn't even happened? Well, you might ask. But what we want you to do here is to use your imagination and do a little crystal ball gazing. We want you to try to forecast your future. We want you to imagine what your life's going to be like in the future. And the answers that you write down to these questions are given a special name — they're your **predictions**.

Will your best subjects at school in the future be the ones you're best at now and name them:

Will you go to college or university after school:

What will your training be after school:

What job do you see yourself doing when you start work:

Where will you be working:

Where will you be living:

Where do you think you'll be spending your summer holidays:

What sort of car or motor-bike will you be
driving:

How old will you be when you get married:

Who do you think you're going to marry:

What do you think your husband, or wife, will look like:

How many children do you think you will have:

What do you think your greatest achievement in life will be (will it be in your work; in your family life; in one of your hobbies; or in some other field):

Will you do a lot of travelling when you get older? If you think you will, which countries do you think you'll visit:

What will your main interests be when you're grown up:

What will you be best at:

Use this page to draw your own portrait in twenty years time. Then put the book somewhere safe and take it out when the time falls due and see how right you were about your appearance and about everything else that you predicted!

BOOKS TO HELP YOU

You probably won't need to look up anything in answering these questions — but just in case you do, here are a few tips for where to turn for help.

Any **children's encyclopaedia** will be able to answer most of your questions about anything. If you don't have one at school, they'll be one at the local library, in the reference section.

You might find an **atlas** useful too. But if you do use one, make sure that it's up-to-date. The shape of the world may not change overnight, but the names of some of the countries do.

There's a very useful book on science, technology and everything to do with knowledge in fact. This is called the *Everyman's Scientific Facts and Feats* and it was written by two leading scientists named Magnus Pyke and Patrick Moore. *The Guinness Book of Answers* has got answers to most things under the sun and again you'll find that in a library.

But, as we said, the aim of the book is for you to test your own knowledge. So don't go rushing to other books for help unless you really have to. After all this is **your** book, so you'll want to fill it in yourself, won't you. (How about answering **every** question before you even think about another book. If you use a pencil you can ink the answers in later and a guess is better than no answer at all!)

CHALLENGE
by GYLES BRANDRETH; ILLUS. PETER STEVENSON

Can YOU eat a bowl of soup with a fork?

Can YOU blow a bubble to beat the world bubble gum record?

Can YOU put on every single pair of socks you own – one after the other?

Can YOU do up your buttons, peel a banana and comb your hair without using your thumbs?

Challenges of journeys, challenges for rainy days, challenges alone and challenges with friends – treasure hunts, brain busters, puzzles, tricks and daredevil dares – can you take a CHALLENGE?

0 552 54194 X   85p

CRAZY DAYS
by GYLES BRANDRETH; ILLUS. PETER STEVENSON

BUDGIE DAY IN Cedar Rapids, U.S.A., 13th January

HIPPO DAY 25th May 1850 – The first hippor arrived in Great Britain

A COLD DAY FOR PEAS 6th March 1930 when frozen foods first appeared in the shops

BALLOON BURSTING DAY 19th July

Make a date with CRAZY DAYS for festive feasts, birthday beanos, anniversaries, jokes and riddles, tongue-twisters and astounding facts to celebrate the whole year through!

What's today's crazy day . . .?

0 552 54191 5   85p

SHADOW SHOWS
by GYLES BRANDRETH; ILLUS. DAVID FARRIS.

Create a tremendous shadow spectacular with thrilling hand shadow techniques, puppets to make, prehistoric monster creations, mysterious magic and illusions, shadow plays and pantomines, and shadow characters to amaze and delight your audience.

Stage and screen settings, lighting, scripts, special effects, props and all the tricks of the trade are included in this superb shadow extravaganza – so dim the lights and let the show begin. . .

0 552 54192 3   85p

THE CRAZY WORD BOOK
by GYLES BRANDRETH; ILLUS. JACQUI
SINCLAIR

From amazing A to zippy Z – this magnificent hotchpotch
of word power and fun will take your brain cells by storm!

Dabble with homophones, agonise over anagrams, astound
a friend with a nippy palindrome, mix up a mnemonic
memory booster, and cross swords with crosswords.

Word pictures, word squares, word games, word codes and
word quizzes galore – become a wordomaniac with this
crazy, crazy word book!!!

0 552 54182 6   75p

THE BIG BOOK OF MAGIC
by GYLES BRANDRETH; ILLUS. PETER
STEVENSON

Presenting, among a treasury of flabbergasting feats and
sleights-of-hand, that mind-boggling stupendous trick –

BOTTLING EGGS!

Take one egg, some vinegar and a bottle. Have the egg
sitting on top of the bottle, and then announce – and
proceed to demonstrate – that you can *get the egg inside the
bottle without breaking the shell!*

How is it done? That's the secret! And if you don't want egg
on your face, careful study of this wondrous volume,
crammed with tricks, aids and hints to inspire awe and
admiration, will produce magical results!!!

0 552 54177 X   80p

THE CRAZY ENCYCLOPAEDIA
by GYLES BRANDRETH; ILLUS. BOBBIE CRAIG

AN A-TO-Z OF TOTAL LUNACY!

COMPILED BY CRACKPOTS!

TELLS YOU NOTHING YOU EVER WANTED TO KNOW!

GUARANTEED USELESS!

NO OTHER ENCYCLOPAEDIA LIKE IT!

ANCIENT JOKES, BRAIN BOGGLERS, DAFFYNI-TIONS, IGNORANCE, KNOCK KNOCKS, NOLEDGE, ODES AND ENDS, SPORTS, TWERPSICHORE, U.F.O.s, WITCHES AND WIZARDS, and CRAZY X,Y,Z. . . . .

0 552 54174 5   75p

THE CRAZY BOOK OF WORLD RECORDS
by GYLES BRANDRETH; ILLUS. MIKE MILLER

Are you a record breaker?

CAN YOU –

* balance more than seven golf balls on top of each other?

* stand on one leg for more than 19 hours?

* shell 12 hard-hoiled eggs in less than 1 minute 59 seconds?

* write a sentence containing over 908 three-lettered words?

* slice a 2 lb onion into more than 157 slices?

These and many more flabbergasting feats and incredible firsts set down by young people all over the world will amaze, astound and, best of all, challenge YOU to be a world-class, number one record winner, too. . . .

0 552 54196 6   85p

THE DAFT DICTIONARY
by GYLES BRANDRETH; ILLUS. IAN WEST

An A-Z of ordinary words with quite extraordinary meanings!

Hundreds of unique daffynitions!!!

D entist: someone who always looks down in the mouth.

A ppear: something you fish off.

F leece: insects that get into your wool if you don't wash properly.

T axidermist: a stuffed cab driver.

H ippies: the things you hang your leggies on.

I llegal: a sick bird of prey

No other dictionary like it in the world!!!!!

0 552 54128 1   60p

THE BIG BOOK OF OPTICAL ILLUSIONS
by GYLES BRANDRETH; ILLUSIONS ALBERT
MURPHY

If you dare to open a copy of this unbelievable book, be
prepared for moving specks before your eyes, grey spots
that appear and disappear, solid objects that cannot exist,
straight lines that wave and bend, gyrating circles, pulsating
patterns and mazes that muddle the mind!

DO NOT believe anything you see. . . . DO NOT attempt
to read this book with a weak stomach. . . . YOU HAVE
BEEN WARNED. . . .

0 552 54155 9   65p

If you would like to receive a newsletter telling you
about our new children's books, fill in the coupon
with your name and address and send it to:

Gillian Osband,

Transworld Publishers Ltd,

Century House,

61-63 Uxbridge Road, Ealing,

London, W5 5SA

Name ....

Address ....

....

CHILDREN'S NEWSLETTER

All the books on the previous pages are available at your
bookshop or can be ordered direct from Transworld Publishers Ltd., Cash Sales Dept. P.O. Box 11, Falmouth,
Cornwall.

Please send full name and address together with cheque
or postal order—no currency, and allow 45p per book
to cover postage and packing (plus 20p each for additional
copies).